Scentwork: Step by Step

Sara Seymour

ISBN: 9798709724105

About The Author

Sara is the owner of Compass Canine, based in Totnes, South Devon. Her primary business is hydrotherapy and canine fitness. She also offers scentwork training, as well as running scentwork events. Sara is an instructor, judge and trial manager for Scentwork UK and hosts Nosework Games events. She currently has one dog, Ripley, a six-year-old working cocker spaniel. Ripley is the embodiment of the saying 'You don't get the dog you want, you get the dog you need'. She has nearly worked out what it was she needed… Her previous dogs include Oscar, a border collie, and Vinnie, an English springer spaniel.

Sara's dog training background was mainly in agility, but these days her training with Ripley, other than scentwork, focuses on Rally obedience. This is mostly online, due to the limited number of 'real life' competitions available. They also enjoy training tricks and a variety of concepts such as mimicry. Sara is training to become a Certified Professional Canine Fitness Trainer (CPCFT). Her training philosophy is best described as 'Do No Harm', and focuses on positive reinforcement-based training that is adapted to each learner. She aims to apply this to both people and dogs.

Sara lives with her husband, John, who is generally introduced as being scared of dogs. However, he has been known to appear at events helping out as needed, desperately trying to remember names and get their pronunciation correct.

1 Ripley and Vinnie

CONTENTS

Acknowledgements

Firstly, thank you to Gwen Johnson for putting on the Train the Trainers event that introduced us to scentwork and Scentwork UK. Also, for all the work you did with me over the following years to help me and Ripley improve, and especially the revelations about the right reinforcement strategy.

That first course was taught by Heather Donnelly, who is behind Scentwork UK along with her team. She also trained me as a judge and trial manager at a later time.

Leanne Smith definitely deserves a mention as I am quite sure that she's a big part of the reason that Ripley is possible to live with and train.

I owe a great deal of gratitude to Julie Daniels. Not only did she introduce us to our beloved Cookie Jar, but she also put a huge amount of faith and trust in me that allowed me to develop as a trainer. I've also borrowed, with her permission, the phrase 'vary the variables'.

Julie Symons sparked my love of Going to Source, and introduced us to some of our favourite sniffing games.

It was after taking Lucy Newton's course on indications that Ripley and I finally started making progress in this element of scentwork, and I was also able to then formulate a process to work through with the owners I train.

The chapter title 'Play is Magic' was inspired by Dr Amy Cook.

She really helped me learn how to play with Ripley in a way that we both enjoy, and her Play Way program is second to none for helping dogs using play.

This book would not have come into existence without the help and support of Sally Smith of Canine Principles. When I signed up for the book writing course that she offered I didn't even know what I was going to write a book about! Thank you Sally, and all of my classmates for the support and belief; I wouldn't be writing this without you.

A big thank you must go to Kathryn Treeby and Debra Cassidy for their help in proof-reading and sense checking the contents that follow.

Finally – thank you to all those that have kept me company and cheered me on along the way. If I start naming individuals I know I'll miss someone, but you all know who you are. Your support is appreciated, and I look forward to continuing spending time with you all.

FOREWORD by Andrew Hale

Our understanding of dogs and their behaviour is constantly evolving. We now have a wider appreciation, supported by science, of their emotional and processing needs. The more we can learn about, and then support, the dogs emotional experience, the closer our bonds become and the better quality of life we can afford them.

One area that has come under a lot of attention in recent years is that of olfaction (the sense of smell). We have known that dogs have an amazing sense of smell for a long time, but the true wonder and indeed importance of this is only now becoming clear.

A big part of a dog's emotional experience is their ability to process information from the world around them. The olfactory process is crucial in this, yet we often stop them from fully sniffing out the world around them. Through most of the traditional training we do with our dogs, we are asking them to 'look at this' or 'listen to that', asking them to primarily use their eyes and ears. This means that sometimes their primary sensory input is being overlooked and even discouraged.

We find lots of outlets for our dogs to engage with through training, but they are often at the expense of them using their noses. Engaging in scentwork is a great way to include their sense of smell in the process. Scentwork has so many positives in relation to the dog's wellbeing and emotional experience and should form a part of a dog's weekly activities with their care givers. It is also important to remember to allow our dogs the need to process through smell whenever they need to, including on the walk – let them sniff!

Scentwork: Step by Step offers you a great way to learn how to include your dog's nose in the activities you do together. Sara has cleverly deconstructed scentwork into its component parts in this book and guides you through the best ways to enjoy this wonderful activity with your dog – one that is totally nose focused! Scentwork is a great way to allow dogs a chance to enjoy processing in a way that is natural and fun. It is a great decompressor for dogs that have a more gentle or anxious disposition. It is low impact for those dogs that have physical ailments. It is almost like a doggy form of mindfulness – allowing the dog to be totally present in the moment as they work to seek out the smells together with you.

I can assure you your dog will thank you for learning more ways to help them engage that wonderful nose of theirs.

Andrew Hale is a Certified Animal Behaviourist based in the UK. He is a trustee of the Association of INTODogs and the behaviour consultant for Pet Remedy.

1 INTRODUCTION AND WHY SCENTWORK

Introduction

My scentwork journey started because my older dog at the time, Vinnie, was retired quite young from agility due to a number of physical issues. He still needed a 'job', but one that was a little less active. As luck would have it, the opportunity came up at around that time to attend a Scentwork UK (SWUK) 'Train the Trainer' workshop locally. Local workshops like this are rare. I actually lent Vinnie to a friend for that workshop, and worked my young dog, Ripley, myself. Training completed, I went away and spent a few weeks working through the exercises with both of my dogs before setting up a series of classes to teach others.

Around this time I also started coming to terms with the fact that agility wasn't really for Ripley – his joy and enthusiasm for working with me doing scentwork was on a whole different scale. This is his super power! I've continued my scentwork learning ever since; my process has evolved since those early days, as has my understanding of what is needed to succeed.

Sadly I lost Vinnie to a very sudden and brief illness in October 2020. Just ten days earlier he had happily worked for another handler at a Nosework Games event as her dog was injured. They even managed to win a rosette together. Ripley is having a successful scentwork career; he has achieved Excellent awards at both Level 1 and Level 2 of Scentwork UK and has qualified a couple of times at Level 3. He gained two third places and an overall third at our first (and only so far!) Nosework Games competition. Once competitions resume, we plan to progress further.

Having seen the impact that scentwork can have on a variety of different dogs, I want to share it with as many people as possible. There are many in-person and online courses available, but people have told me that they would like a basic book to work with – so here I am, writing my first book. Thank you for reading it; I hope that you and your canine companions get as much pleasure from scentwork as we do.

There are two main skill sets that we need to teach in order to succeed with scentwork: indicating and searching. These two skill sets are broken down in to a number of different elements. Within this book I'll walk you through each of these elements, and explain clearly how they all work together. You can go through as many or as few of the steps as you want, and will still be left with a new game to play with your dog. For most people, it will work best if you work through each section as you read it rather than reading the whole book before starting. That said, I know that some people like to see the whole picture and so you could read the whole book, then go back and get started with the training. The format of the book means that it is a resource that you can refer back to as and when you need to fine tune your training.

I wanted to keep the process as simple as possible, so whilst there are some important technical terms I have tried to keep these to a minimum and explain them as clearly as I can. I've included a glossary of the most common terms for you to refer to as needed. My contact details are at the back of the book, so if you do get stuck you can always reach out and ask. I would also highly recommend working with a local trainer if you do ever get stuck or if you decide that you would like to take your scentwork training to the next level.

It's often said that the only thing that two dog trainers can agree on is that the third trainer is wrong. With that in mind, I will say that there are many different ways to train scentwork. In this book I've detailed the approach that I now use, which has developed over the years that I've been training it. It's by no means the only way; it should work for most dogs, but there is NEVER a one size fits all approach in dog training. So if you get started, get stuck and seek out help then don't be concerned if the trainer has a slightly different approach. It doesn't mean that either of us is more right or wrong than the other; we just have different learning histories.

I've included a chapter at the end of the book with some further challenges to try with your dog once you've completed the scentwork training detailed in the book. These are all inspired by the challenges that I set in the Scentwork Online Challenges Facebook Group – you can join that group to see video examples.

If you would like more videos and support with your training, then I have a self-study course offered through a Facebook group. You can contact me through my website, www.compasscanine.co.uk. I also post training videos on both my Compass Canine Scentwork Facebook page and Ripley's Facebook and Instagram pages, both called Talented Mr Rip.

Why Scentwork?

Scentwork is a hugely beneficial activity for our canine companions. The part of their brain that analyses and processes scent is about 40% greater than ours. It's been estimated that dogs can smell anywhere between 1000 and 10,000 times better than humans. Whilst we rely primarily on our sight, dogs see the world through their noses – this is why they often cope well with losing their sight as they age (and why sometimes we don't even realise).

The fact that using their nose means that they're using a large part of their brain leads to scentwork being more mentally tiring than other training activities. Mental activity is as important, if not more, than physical activity for our dogs. I may not walk my dog every day, but I do some form of training, even if only for five to ten minutes. Scentwork activities are so simple to add in to your day, and you will notice the benefits.

You can take your scentwork journey as far as you would like; it can be a fun activity to do with your dog and the family, or you can enter competitions. There are a few organisations that run scentwork trials of some sort in the UK. The two that I have experience of are Scentwork UK and Nosework Games. The training contained in this book will give you a solid foundation in order to be able to enter trials with either of these.

For those who are already experienced trainers, I hope that you too will find a gem or two in the book. I'm a lifelong learner, and never fail to pick up something new when interacting with a different trainer. If nothing else, going back to basics is often fun for both us and our dogs.

2 BEFORE YOU BEGIN

In this chapter I'll go over some of things that you will need to know and to prepare before you get started with your training. This includes equipment, treats, clicker training, play and scent preparation and handling.

Equipment

Detailed below are some of the supplies that you will need to get started with your training.

For scent:

Scent jars – I like wide, squat jars. For example, the ones you get containing salsa or sour cream dips. You will need at least two – one for your scent, and one for 'blanks'.

Sock pieces – rather than throw away your holey socks, pop them in the wash and save them for scent. Cut them up into pieces about 1" (2.5cm) square. If you really want, you could buy new socks just for scentwork. These are known as 'soaks'.

Velcro (optional) – as we progress, it's sometimes easier to use the sticky backed Velcro. However, this isn't essential.

Cloves – whole cloves, that you buy from the spice section in the supermarket. We'll be using cloves as that is the initial scent used in both Scentwork UK and Nosework Games.

Gloves – Latex type disposable ones; you'll need these for 'clean' handling of scent.

Tweezers – again, these are used for clean handling of scent.

Scent holders (optional) – small containers for soaks can be really useful to avoid contamination and also to easily take your searching on the road. Examples include histology cassettes and centrifuge test tube vials. These are relatively inexpensive to buy in bulk, so it may be best to group together with a couple of friends if you don't want hundreds of each. Alternatively, you can buy in smaller quantities from the suppliers detailed at the back of the book.

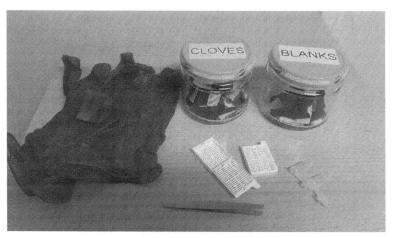

2 Scent jars, gloves, tweezers and cases

For indications:

Yoghurt/porridge pots – you will need a pot of some sort that is big enough for your dog to stick his nose in. I find that the instant porridge pots suit most dogs, but for smaller dogs the larger, squat yoghurt pots would work. For larger dogs, either a round ice cream tub or a plant pot. You'll need at least three.

Small tin – this is a little more specific, but will come in very handy. The best tins are magnetic spice tins. Having a few will come in handy (luckily, as you can't usually buy just one) – if you have friends that are also working through this book, then it would be worth buying a set and sharing them out. Alternatives would be an empty lip balm tin with some holes drilled in it. There are also companies that sell scentwork supplies, and they are detailed at the back of the book.

3 Empty pots and examples of tins

For searching:

Boxes – a selection of cardboard boxes, shoebox size. Wine or small vegetable boxes from the supermarket are also a good size and shape.

Bags – small backpacks, sports bags or similar. Just one or two.

Plant pots – plastic or terracotta. The terracotta ones are a bit more solid, but best used on a soft surface or grass. You will need five or six of these. For larger dogs you could use buckets. An alternative to plant pots is biscuit tins or sweet tubs with holes poked or drilled in.

Other items – basically the contents of my shed, with a few things sneaked out of the garage when my husband's not looking! Watering cans, bricks, buckets, old wellies – the possibilities are endless in this category.

Treats

Training for scentwork is easiest using food. Once trained, you can certainly use toys if that's what your dog prefers, but to start with we need to use food. I appreciate that this can be an issue for some dogs: those that are having reduced activity, small dogs that can't eat lots, dogs with food intolerances for example. Before we get on to what treats you can use, I want to give a brief overview of where and how you should reward during your scentwork training. I also understand that some people will be cautious about encouraging their dog to eat treats off the floor, worrying that this will mean that they will always be looking for treats on the ground. The key thing to remember here is that we will be putting this behaviour on cue – meaning that we will be telling our dog when to start searching, and also when to stop. Over time they will learn that treats are usually only available for them on the floor when you cue them to search for them. That said, they are by nature opportunistic scavengers so this training alone will not fix any issues you may have in this area!

Rewarding at source – this means that the treats are given at the source of the scent. This is really important in the early stages of introducing scent. If the scent is near the floor, you can pop the treats on the floor as close as possible to the scent. If the scent is hidden higher up, cup one hand next to where the scent is hidden and place treats from your other hand in there for your dog to take. I like to place treats one or two at a time rather than a handful in one go. As you progress and there are times when you are further away from your dog, then you can throw the treats to them – just make sure that they are comfortable with this. At that stage you could also use a toy if they prefer, but be careful not to hit them with it!

Reset treats – these are treats that you throw for your dog to chase. Once they've got the treat, they should turn and return to you so that you can give them another cue or direct them as needed. If you've not already taught this skill to your dog it's worth doing. To start, hold the treat almost on the end of your dog's nose and watch to make sure that they follow it as you throw it just a short distance to start with. I usually say 'get it' as I do this, so that they learn that it's OK to take it. Gradually build up the distance you throw it, and you should also be able to move away from having the treat right in front of their nose to start.

Treats from you - depending on your overall aim, if you decide to try a scentwork competition then you generally won't be able to reward at source. With this in mind, it's worth working on this in training as well. For me, if I use a clicker then I know that Ripley is going to return to me (at speed) to get his treats. I also let him work a lot of the searches independently, meaning I'm often nowhere near him when he gets the find. And I can't throw all that well, so it's easier for us both if the reward comes directly from me. I do work on exercises where I can reward at source, and those are detailed in the Going to Source section.

Treat Ideas

The best treats for scentwork are small, dry, non-crumbly treats. Exactly what will be down to your dogs. I generally use a small-bite, high quality kibble when I need a high volume of treats. If needed, I can adjust the amount of food they get for their meals to ensure they don't gain weight. You may find that the very act of having to work for the food makes something you would consider 'boring' to be the best food in the world in the dog's eyes. I always said that Vinnie would work for cardboard – he just loved to work!

Option 1 – use your dog's daily rations (or part of it) for training. This is a great strategy for all training; it's far more interesting for your dog to work for their food rather than just munch it from a bowl twice a day. You can make their kibble more interesting by popping it in a bag with some chicken or hot dogs for example (I call this 'chick 'n' mix')

Option 2 – if you can't use their meals, make sure that you reduce rations accordingly to take account of the extra calories that they're getting from treats. This option is often a good one for those who feed raw or wet food of some sort.

Option 3 – look for high quality, low fat treats. There are many options available now. I prefer single protein treats for my dogs – no added rubbish. I'll pop a link in the References and Resources section at the back to the company that sells these treats. If you're local to me in Sunny South Devon, then I supply many of them.

Option 4 – make your own treats! There are many, many recipes online. By making your own, you will know exactly what is in there. One of the easiest I make is tuna cake – this can be cooked in the microwave and finished off in the oven if needed. In fact, you can use the same basic recipe with any sort of protein (leftover meat, for example). I'm no Delia, but my basic recipe is below.

Basic treat recipe:

In a blender, whizz together a tin of tuna with a couple of eggs and a little water, oil (any type will do) or milk. Once smooth, add in a little flour (I use rice flour usually). You're aiming for a pancake batter consistency if you have moulds, a little thicker if not. I use '160' ice cube trays to bake mine in – saves a whole lot of time cutting them up! Cook in the microwave until firm. If you would like them a little drier, then spread on a baking tray and put in the oven on 70° until they have dried out – it's hard to overdo them unless you leave them in there and go on holiday for a fortnight! These can be frozen once cooked if needed.

Play is Magic

Play is a really important part of any training you do with your dog. Studies have shown that including play in our training sessions with our dogs can help to improve their memory. Besides, it's fun!

There are three main categories of play: food play, toy play and personal play. Play is a complex topic which could warrant a book of its own, so for now I'll cover a small amount of detail of each below. In essence though, I would highly recommend that you end your sessions with a little bit of play – whichever type works best for you and your dog in that moment. This will really help to condition a positive emotional response in your dog to your training sessions.

Food play – It's OK to play with your food! There are lots of games you can play with treats that are far more interesting than just giving it to your dog. Options include tossing individual treats for them to chase, throwing treats for your dog to catch (or not catch as is so often the case), sprinkling a number of treats around on the floor or moving the treat around in your hand for your dog to chase. I regularly end sessions with a scatter (I call it 'sprinkles') as this brings Ripley's energy down and enables him to transition to settling more easily after a session. However, this will often be after I've thrown treats for him to chase or tossed a few for him to catch. Or drop. We have good days and bad days with that one! With scentwork and sniffing being so rewarding for Ripley, I regularly make the rewarding afterwards last at least as long as the time he was searching.

Toy play – there are a few options with toys. Some dogs enjoy playing tug, others like to chase a ball and there are those that just want to catch and hold a ball. Vinnie would have sold his soul for a tennis ball, and mostly he just liked to parade around with it. Once in a while he would throw it at someone's feet and try to persuade them to throw it. Ripley enjoys tug, but not all the time. I often offer a toy at the end of a training session to give him the option. He does also like to parade around with the toy, 'killing' it as he does. As a rehab professional, the only word of caution that I would give is against repetitive throwing. One or two throws is fine, but not half an hour of back and forth.

Personal play – this is very personal to each dog. Some dogs would rather not be touched, and that should always be respected. There are those that enjoy some calm stroking, chin scratches and belly rubs. Then there's dogs like Ripley that like a bit of rough and tumble play fighting. You can work out what your dog enjoys most by either watching them with other dogs or trying a few things out. I'd also suggest checking out Dr Amy Cook and the Play Way to discover even more about personal play.

Each of the different types of play can be combined, so that you do a little bit of each, or you can just pick one that you prefer. What you choose may also depend on the environment that you're training in and what you're trying to achieve. If I've trained something that requires a lot of self control and thought on the dog's part, then I'm likely to end with some more energetic play to allow them to release some of the energy that they've been holding back. If we've been working on something high energy, then I'll use some calm personal play or food scatters to bring that energy down. I'm always looking for some sort of balance.

Try a few things out with your dog and see what they enjoy. Take your play on walks; it will help to build engagement and strengthen your relationship with your dog.

Handling and Preparing Scent

Now that you've gathered your equipment, it's time to prepare your scent. Although we won't be using this straight away it's worthwhile getting it ready so that it's there when we need it.

In one of your jars, place ten to twelve of the cut-up sock pieces and add in about fifteen cloves. Pop the lid on and leave it for a couple of days. These pieces of sock, often referred to as 'soaks', will absorb the scent of the cloves. Best practise is to only use each soak once; just top up your jar from time to time with new sock pieces or Velcro. It's always a good idea to label your jars so that you don't mix things up.

In the other jar, just add sock pieces. These sock pieces will be 'blanks'. Using blanks in your searches ensures that your dog is learning just the clove scent and not learning to look for sock pieces. I'll cover this in more detail later in the book.

When handling scent, you should try to use either tweezers or gloves. Avoid touching items with your gloves after you have handled a soak. This is to avoid getting traces of your scent or the target scent onto objects, as that could confuse your dog.

Scent handling is important, especially if you want to get to a stage where you could take your dog to a competition. However, if you are looking to do it just for fun, or a bit of a party trick, then you can be a little less cautious (just don't tell anyone I said that!)

There is a lot to be mindful of when it comes to handling and dealing with scent. There are trainers and handlers who will be extra-cautious, and certainly they need to be when their dogs are going to be operational (i.e., working in real-life situations). We can learn a great deal from these handlers, but at the same time I don't want you to be overwhelmed or put off by some of the precautions and suggestions that I make. You will get a feel for what works well for your dog, and what they can and can't deal with. Certainly, my scent handling hasn't always been as clean as it is now (and even now I cut corners if I'm just doing some quick training with Ripley). Please don't worry too much about it, but just be aware of the tips that I give throughout, even if they do get repetitive.

Clicker Training

I am sure that many of you will be aware of 'clicker training', sometimes referred to as 'marker training'. It turned up in Jurassic Park, and Sheldon used the technique with Penny in an episode of the Big Bang Theory. I've been using a clicker in my dog training for over twenty years now. It's an incredibly effective and efficient way of training.

That said, it's not necessary for scentwork. I will include clicker training options, but will also explain how to train the exercises without a clicker. If you want a brief summary of what clicker training is, and how it works, then please read on. If not, go ahead and jump to the next section.

There are a variety of different styles of clicker, but basically they all make a clicking noise when pressed. When you first start out, this clicking sound is meaningless to your learner. The power of the clicker comes from pairing it with reinforcement. For simplicity's sake, the example I'll use will have food as our reinforcer.

To introduce the clicker, and help your dog understand what it means, you can use the following process (this is often referred to as 'charging the clicker'):

Click, pause, give treat

Repeat this five to ten times – by that point, you should see a reaction from your dog when you click; they are now anticipating that the sound means they are going to get a treat! IMPORTANT – you need to make sure that there is a pause between your click and giving the treat, just a quick count of one. This makes sure that the dog is noticing the click, and not just focussing on the food. Once you see that the dog is reacting to the click, you can move to the next step – they need to do something to make you click. A simple example would be eye contact, or focus on your face. Toss a treat away from you – as your dog turns back, after they've eaten the treat, wait for them to start to look up to you and CLICK. Hand them one treat, and then toss another one away to start another repetition.

Think of the clicker like a camera – the click is you capturing that moment in time, telling the dog that what they did at that moment is what earned them a treat. You need to get the treat to them fairly quickly, but try not to rush. Just bear in mind that anything that happens between the click and them getting the treat is also reinforced – this is why Ripley puts his feet up on me after I click his scentwork indication. As an alternative to a clicker, you can use a marker word, such as 'yes' – this serves a similar purpose to the clicker, and works on the same principle. The advantage of a clicker over a verbal marker is that the dog's brain processes the click sound ever so slightly more quickly.

For the purposes of this book, I don't want to go into much more detail about clicker training. There are a large number of resources available, both free and paid, and I'll include some of these in the References section at the end of the book. Throughout I will refer to 'marking' your dog, and by that I mean either with a clicker or with a word as described above.

3 GLOSSARY OF TERMS

I'll list below a number of terms that occur frequently throughout the book, along with their definitions within the context of this book.

Blanks – these are sock pieces or Velcro that have no scent on them.

Blind hides – hides where the dog doesn't know where the scent is hidden. Could also be when the handler doesn't know where the hide is.

Clean item – an item that has either never been scented or has been thoroughly cleaned after being scented.

Cue – usually a word or hand signal that prompts your dog to perform a particular behaviour.

Hide – the place or item where your scent has been placed.

Hot item – an item that has been scented.

Indication – how your dog shows you that they've found the scent.

In Odour/Scent – this is where your dog has picked up the target scent whilst searching, and are then working towards the source

Mark or marker – this can be either a clicker or word; it's the sound that is made at the moment that your dog does something correct.

On Odour – this means that your dog has learned a target odour, and they can work their searches to find that scent rather than just searching for treats.

Play – this can be with food, toys or just you.

Reward – can be food, toy or play.

Scent – interchangeable with odour, for the purposes of this book this will refer to the clove scent that you'll be using.

Soaks – these are the sock pieces or Velcro that are kept in your scent jars to soak up the scent.

Source – the exact spot where the scent is hidden.

Target scent – in this book, our target scent is cloves. This could also be referred to as target odour.

Task - To task your dog, start with your hand just in front of the dog's nose with your palm open and facing their nose. Sweep your hand towards your start point as though you are drawing a line from your dog's nose to the start point. Allow your dog to follow your hand in a slow controlled movement.

Vary the variables – think about the things that you can change in your set up and vary. Try to only change one thing at a time to start with to help your dog succeed.

4 AN OVERVIEW OF THE SEARCHES

As I've mentioned before, the main organisations with which I have experience of competing are Scentwork UK and Nosework Games. When teaching scentwork to someone that is new to it, I find it useful to explain the searches that you would come across in these competitions so that you know what we are aiming towards. If you don't intend to compete, then you could skip this section or come back to it later for inspiration.

Scentwork UK:

There are five possible searches in the first four levels – Boxes and Bags, Exterior, Tables and Chairs, Vehicles and Walls. However, you will only complete four searches as the competition will include either a Vehicle, a Wall OR a combination of a Vehicle and Wall. Further details of this are covered later in the book.

Boxes and Bags (sometimes referred to as Containers) – generally undertaken inside, this search area is made up of five or six boxes plus five or six bags. The boxes can be cardboard, plastic or other materials. Usually at Level 1 the boxes will be open. At Level 1 the odour will be in either a box or a bag, and there's just one hide to find.

4 An example of a Boxes & Bags search layout

Tables and Chairs – another indoor search. There will be two tables and eight chairs, and the scent at the lower levels will be on a chair. The tables and chairs will be arranged in a canteen sort of style, e.g. a table with two chairs on either side, or one on each side if it's a smaller table.

5 A typical Tables & Chairs search layout

Exterior items – this is the contents of your shed, as described in the equipment list. There will be twelve to fifteen items, randomly arranged. At Level 1, you will get the option of being told three items that the hide could be in (you should still set out to search all items, not just those three).

6 Exterior search layout example

The fourth search will be either a vehicle, a wall or a combination of vehicles and walls.

Vehicle – the number of vehicles will depend on the level, just one at Level 1. The hide will be on the exterior of the car, and should be low enough for the dog to find without jumping up on the car (as we don't want to damage our cars).

Wall – the length of the wall will depend on the level, and also whether it's being combined with a vehicle search.

7 An example of a vehicle and wall search area

For each search there is a set time limit, which depends on the level. The times are fairly generous though. All of the searches can be worked with the dog either on a lead or off lead. If using a lead, I would highly recommend that you use a harness rather than collar, as there is potential to cause damage to their neck if your dog pulls too hard in to a collar. For full details and rules, please visit the Scentwork UK website, which is www.scentworkuk.com

Nosework Games:

Nosework Games are much newer than Scentwork UK, and rapidly developing. There are currently nine games, each designed to test different skills needed for a successful scentwork team. Full details are on their website, www.noseworkgames.uk

Adopt a Position – set up in a square with the handler in the middle, there will be one hide along each side. The four positions that you will send your dog from are sitting in a chair, standing in a marked area, standing with your hands behind your back and organiser's choice (at my Christmas event I had the owners singing Jingle Bells whilst their dogs searched!)

8 Adopt a Position, with Ripley ready to play

Darts – there will be four 'targets' and you need to pick three that you'll send your dog to. You need to stay on a set point when sending your dog, and the points awarded will depend on the perceived difficulty of the hide.

Distance – in this game, there are a known number of hides, and they will be at increasing distances. The handler needs to stay behind the start line, with the dog heading out to search independently.

9 Items set out at increasing distances

Go to Source – a number of stations will be set up of similar items (e.g. crates, chairs). These items will have numbers placed on them, which are places where the odour could be hidden. The goal here is not just to find the correct item, but exactly WHERE on the item the hide is.

10 Each station has multiple areas numbered where the scent could be

Hidden Treasures – this is a container search, but the containers will be filled with either water, soil or sand. The number of hides will be unknown, so you will have to call the area clear once you think your dog has found them all.

11 These buckets contain water for a Hidden Treasures search

Line Ups – this game is worked on a lead, and sees a number of rows with five or six similar items in each row. You can work each line up and back ONCE. Some lines could be blank, and you won't know in advance how many hides you are looking for. At most there will be one hide per line.

12 Five lines ready to be searched

Needle in a Haystack – for this game, there will be a LOT of items to search, with a relatively low number of hides. You will be told how many hides there are. This game is worked off lead.

13 A high number of items with multiple hides

Snake – similar to line ups, this one is worked on lead. This will be a long continuous line of items, in an 'S' shape for example. You can only work along the line once.

14 An example of a Snake set up

Speed – again, there will be a high number of hides to find. However, the time you have will be quite short and the area could be busy, with lots of items to search or a larger space. This is another off lead search.

You can see more details of the games, as well as video examples, on the Nosework Games – Competitors Facebook page.

5 HOW TO USE THIS BOOK

As previously mentioned, there are two main elements that I will be teaching you in this book: indicating and searching. Each skill is broken down into steps. You can, and probably should, work on the indication and the searching at the same time – BUT NOT IN THE SAME SESSION.

I explained earlier that scentwork can be tiring for our dogs. A lot of their brain goes into this, so in the learning stages we want to make it as easy as we can. So in one session you could work on some searching, and then you can work on the indication in a separate session. This could be later on the same day, or even on a different day – alternate between them.

It's also important in the early stages that you don't work on this every day. Give your dog a break; this will also allow latent learning to take place. Latent learning is what happens between sessions – it's the reason that you can try and train something, and feel like you're making no progress, then come back a few days later to find that they just 'get' it. Take advantage of this!

You may find that the two skill sets progress at different rates – don't panic, this is normal. Just keep working through the steps and it will all come together in the end. Remember to try things in different places (more detail on this in the coming chapters). The more you do this, the happier your dog will be to work in different environments.

Please, please – TAKE YOUR TIME! This isn't a race. It is far better to do a few short training sessions than to do one long session. Ideally, only train for five to ten minutes at a time before taking a break. You could set a timer, or count out a set number of treats. This should help to avoid doing 'just one more rep'. Don't be caught out by wanting to end on a good note – sometimes trying to get a good repetition results in lots of bad ones first. If something goes wrong, just ask your dog for an easy behaviour that they know well, reward them for that and then take a break or move on. We really want them to be successful and have positive feelings about working with us.

Watch out for signs of fatigue from your dog – this is tiring work, and we don't want to push them too far. If your dog is looking distracted where previously they were engaged, then you've probably gone on too long. If they are acting like an overtired toddler, you've probably gone on too long. As I say above, keep the sessions short. Finish them before your dog runs out of steam.

Try to take some video – video is so important in improving our training. Sometimes we're so wrapped up in focusing on one element, we miss other things that are going on. You may be scratching your head about something in the moment, but when you watch the video back it becomes clear what happened. I've included a picture below of a really simple stand for your phone using the cardboard tube from a toilet roll. No excuses! Honestly, the more you video, the less conscious you will be about it; there's no need to share the videos (although you may want to eventually), and you can delete it straight after you review it if you want.

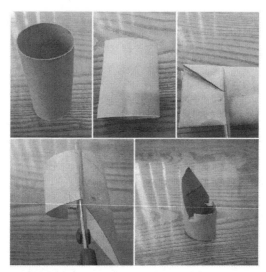

15 How to make a phone holder from a toilet roll inner tube

When I first started scentwork, we taught our dogs to search first and then added an indication later. I now believe that the indication training should come much earlier; indeed, this is how most professionals train these days. So the indication steps are laid out first. That said, you don't need to have gone all the way through them before you start on the searching exercises. However, you should make sure that you have completed ALL the indication steps before you introduce scent to your searches. This will avoid confusion for your dog in the long run.

You are going to need to think of a couple of new cues for your dog – I will let you know when to use these, but it's worth having a think in advance about the words you want to use.

Search cue – this will be the word that you use to ask your dog to search. This word has a BIG meaning! Eventually, this one word will mean 'search the area and/or items for the target odour and give an indication when you find it'. That's quite a lot in one little word! I use the word 'search'. Other options I've heard are 'go sniff' and 'find it'. Ultimately, the actual word doesn't matter, as long as you are consistent in its use. You do want to make sure that you use this word ONLY for your scentwork – please don't use a word that you already use for something else, such as finding a toy. This needs to be a unique word just for this. Write down some of your options in the box below – try them out on your own, and see which feel most natural or comfortable to you.

All done cue – this is a cue to let your dog know that they should stop searching; there's either nothing left to find, or you've run out of time. We introduce this cue almost straight away, so you need to have it picked out before you start any training. I use 'all done', but other options are 'finished' or 'that'll do'. Again, write down your options and try a few out before you get started.

There are times that you will need to place items and treats without your dog helping, but whilst they can see what you're doing. There are a few options for handling this. If your dog will sit and wait, then that's great – but not if you have to repeatedly tell them to stay or keep putting them back. Having a helper is perfect; either they can hold the dog whilst you set things up, or they can set the area up whilst you hold your dog. You could use a mat or platform for your dog to wait on, again so long as you don't need to nag them or keep resetting them. Another option is to attach their lead to something secure. Please have a think about how you are going to handle this element before you get started, and maybe practice a little bit with your dog.

Include play in your sessions; at any time things aren't quite working the way you would like, switch to some play, take a break and try again. End each session with a little bit of play. It will make a difference.

I have given you space throughout to take notes, and provided some questions and thinking points for those notes. Please do make use of these to help your training progress.

Knowing that not everything always goes to plan with our canine companions, I have included a brief 'What Should I Do If My Dog...' chapter towards the end of the book. Go ahead and skip to this one any time you think you need to.

I will warn you now that there is some repetition in the book, but some things are so important that they need to be said a number of times. Rather than refer you back to previous or future sections, I just go ahead and say it all again.

6 INDICATION

An indication is the way that your dog lets you know that they have found the target scent. Sometimes it's called an alert. Indications are split into two categories: active and passive.

Active indications – examples of active indications are barking or pawing at a hide. An active indication such as barking is often used with dogs searching for human remains; if a dog is on a boat carrying out a search of the water, then a passive indication is impractical (and yes, dogs can detect scent that is underwater).

Passive indications – these include nose touches, sits, downs or freezes. These are used when dealing with explosives, for example. The dog finds the source of the odour and stays with it until released by the handler.

When I was first taught scentwork, we were encouraged to see what sort of alert behaviour our dogs naturally offered and build on that. Whilst this approach is fine for a lot of dogs, it can cause problems depending on their preferred behaviours. Vinnie chose to use his feet, tapping or scratching at the hide. This got more enthusiastic as he got more excited; not great if the hide is on someone's car and I didn't spot his foot going up! Ripley has a strong default retrieve behaviour, so he would try to remove soaks. With both I had taught a reliable 'all done' cue so that I could stop them in their tracks, before they managed too much damage. As we progressed I decided to teach Ripley a chin rest, as this is incompatible with retrieving. This mostly worked, although when he got excited other behaviours did creep in at times (and sniffing is pretty exciting for him!)

Finally, I took a class through Fenzi Dog Sports Academy taught by Lucy Newton that was dedicated to teaching indications. This was a turning point for me, and led me to develop the process that I've detailed below. I worked this through with Ripley, and also started it with Vinnie. The photo on the cover of this book shows Ripley doing his nose touch indication. He held this indication for a while, with me a short distance away, whilst I took a few photos. I'll be the first to admit that he's still a work in progress, and isn't always perfect, but he's a lot better than he was. Knowing that he has a clear way of telling me he's found the scent has taken some of the conflict out of our searches, and because his indications have been so well rewarded he's far more willing to indicate than he has been in the past. Sniffing is so intrinsically rewarding for him that there were times when he would choose to keep searching even if he'd found the scent.

We'll also be using the indication training to introduce the target scent and get our dogs working 'on odour'. Please make sure that you have completed all of the steps in this section before you introduce scent to your searches. Until then, your search training should be for treats only.

So let's get on with the training. Please read through all the steps below first and then get to work. Take your time, and don't be tempted to skip any steps. You can go back and revisit any of the earlier steps at any point in your training. Ripley loves being a demo dog to show people how to do the early stages.

Step 1 – high

Equipment needed – porridge or yoghurt pot, treats, clicker (if using)

Start out in a quiet room where you won't be disturbed. You will probably find it easiest to sit in a chair for this step. The aim of this step is to get your dog putting his nose in the pot, and keep it there for a short while. The reason I use a pot rather than a flat object is twofold: it's easy to ensure that you are consistently marking and rewarding the correct criteria (the nose is either in the pot or it isn't) and the pot is quite an obvious prompt for the dog to work out.

This is definitely easier for some dogs than others. My dogs have a history of being given cream or yoghurt pots to lick out, so they're more than willing to stick their noses in pots! Make sure that your pot is an appropriate size for your dog, you don't want it to be too big or small, and may have to try a couple out before settling on one. For dogs that are nervous about putting their nose in the pot, you can cut a rectangular hole towards the bottom edge that you can pop treats through. This can also help to get them keeping their nose in there once we get to that step.

Using a clicker for this step works well, but can be a bit fiddly as you almost need three hands. You can use a marker word instead – I use 'yes'. It's the same process as with a clicker: behaviour, marker word, very brief pause, treat.

Hold the pot at your dog's nose height, at such an angle as to make it easy for your dog to put their nose in. If this is completely new to them, then mark and reward as soon as they move towards the pot. If they are a bit more confident, then wait for the nose to go in. MARK IMMEDIATELY – we are NOT looking for any sort of duration at this stage. We just want them to get the idea that sticking their nose in the pot is a good thing. I would like you to get at least 100 repetitions of this, but not in one session! This will be over a number of sessions, across a number of days. You can do a few repetitions whilst the kettle boils, or during a TV advert break.

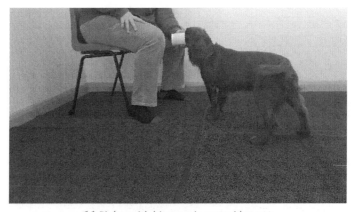

16 Ripley with his nose in a porridge pot

Use the following space to write some notes on how your sessions go – roughly how long did you train for, how many repetitions, etc. Do you feel like you got your mechanics and timing right? Did you video – watch it back and see if what you think was happening matches up with what you see in the video.

Step 2 – low

Equipment needed – pot, treats, clicker (if using), low box or stool

Have you done at least 100 repetitions with the pot at your dog's nose height? Do you promise? You can go back to that step at any time – I still do. Now we want the pot a little lower, but not all the way to the floor. Resting it on a low stool or an upturned box is ideal (and you should have a small collection of boxes by now). The pot should be low enough that your dog can get their nose in it without having to dip their head too much. Keep holding on to the pot for now – you can fade your hand out later. Another option if you're using a box is to cut a hole in it to support the pot. Basically, you don't want it constantly falling over as that could interrupt the flow of the session. Again, you're not looking for any duration at the moment – you just want the nose in the pot. Guess what - I'd like you to do at least 100 repetitions at this height. Split the repetitions over a number of days, I would say at least a week working on this level (and it should have taken around a week to get through the last step as well). An easy way to make sure that you don't do too many repetitions in one session is to count out about ten treats. Once they're gone, end the session.

17 A porridge pot supported in a small cardboard box

Start out working this step whilst sitting down. Once you're getting to the end of your 100 repetitions, try standing up (your pot will need to be quite stable on whatever it's standing on at this point). Don't be surprised if you see a deterioration in your dog's performance: a slight change in the picture can throw them off. Be prepared to accept slightly lower criteria, even just a glance towards the pot. Once they are confident again, then move around a little just so that they get the idea that it doesn't matter where you are, putting their nose in the pot is what gets them paid.

There's more space here for you to take notes (a great habit to get into).

Step 3 – floor

I expect you can work this one out by now! I found that supporting the pot between my feet stopped it from falling over when Ripley got a bit enthusiastic. I would still do this step sitting down to start with. Once you're getting to the end of your 100 repetitions, try standing occasionally as detailed above.

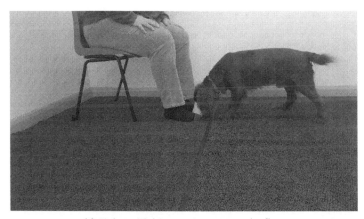

18 Ripley with his nose in a pot on the floor

Have you completed all of these steps? Pop some notes down below about your progress – what was good, what needs more work?

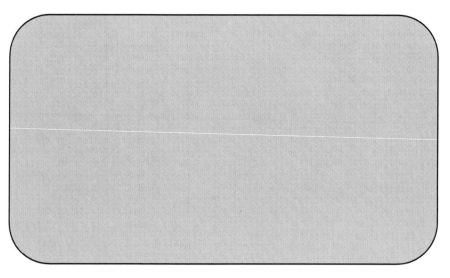

Introducing Scent

Once you've worked through all of the initial indication steps we can start to introduce scent. We'll be pairing the scent with food; basically each time your dog gets their nose on the scent, you'll mark and reward. They will then begin to associate the smell with a reward, making it worth their while to tell you when they've found it.

Before getting started, you'll need to take one of your soaks from your clove jar and tape it to the bottom of your pot. If you've got some sticky-backed Velcro in there, then that's easy to stick to the bottom of the pot. You'll need three pots in total, but only put scent in one of them. Carefully put a 'blank' in one of the other pots. You only need a blank in one pot, it is there to make sure that the only unique thing about the 'hot' pot is the scent. As explained in the chapter on preparing and handling scent, try to avoid directly touching the soak or blank with your hands. If you use gloves to put the soak into a pot, then make sure to use clean gloves for the blank (or place the blank first). This is to avoid contamination.

Step 1 – one pot

To start, do a few repetitions of your dog putting his nose in the pot with the scent in; from now on you will always use scent when working on your indication. After five or six repetitions, put down the other two pots. To make it easy for your dog, make sure that the scented pot is the one closest to them and then mark as soon as they go to sniff it. Next, move the pots around and let your dog sniff them. They may pause at the first one they get to, as that's what has worked in the past. Just wait and give them time to think through the problem – they will probably move on quite quickly. Again, mark as soon as they get to the scented one.

If your dog is rather enthusiastic, then go ahead and cut holes in some small boxes to support the pots.

This is now getting harder for your dog, as they are having to make a choice. It's more important than ever that you keep your sessions short. Multiple short sessions will be more productive than one long session. (I said I'd be repeating myself, but some things definitely bear repeating!)

How did you get on with introducing the scent? Add some notes below, including things that you may need to focus on in your next session.

Step 2 – adding duration

Until now, we haven't really asked for much duration from our dogs. Rather, we've been marking and feeding as soon as their nose goes in the pot. Adding duration should be done very gradually to start with; just pause a fraction of a second longer before marking. Next time, mark immediately again. Ping pong up and down for different durations, e.g. one second, immediate, two seconds, one second, immediate, one second, three seconds, immediate. Like with all the other steps, work on this for five to ten treats and then have a break. Before too long, your dog should be able to keep their nose in the pot for five seconds. Still go back to marking immediately as well though.

If your dog keeps taking their nose out of the pot before you can mark, then you are waiting too long to mark. Try to avoid letting this happen too often, as you don't want them to get into the habit of taking their nose off odour once they've sourced it. Once you have a little duration with one pot, bring in the other two pots so that they have to make a choice. As you're making it harder, don't push for a long duration to start with. Again, ping pong between different lengths of time.

Make notes below from each of your sessions on how much you have built up your duration. Include what your plan is for increasing this in future sessions – what's your aim?

Step 3 – switching to a tin

One of the reasons for switching to a tin is that it's easier to hide once we get to that step. It does also make it a bit harder – no longer a pot to get their nose in! You will need to repeat the first three steps of the indication training above, using your tin. Have odour in it from the start, and you won't need to do as many repetitions as your dog should have a good idea of what the game is now. Try to make sure that you are marking for the nose being on the tin, and not off to one side for example. Also go through the steps for building duration (I usually do this sat down, holding the tin at the dog's nose height to start with).

19 Ripley nose targeting a tin in my hand

As soon as you are happy that your dog is nose targeting your scented tin, you should introduce a couple of other tins so that they have to make a choice. As mentioned in the equipment list, the magnetic spice tins are great for this step as you can pop them on the fridge. Make sure to swap the tins around, and mark immediately to start with. As your dog gets more confident with this exercise you can hold out for a little bit of duration, or even bring in a couple more tins for them to search.

20 If you have magnetic tins, then a fridge is great for starting these searches

That's it – by now, your dog should have a nose freeze on odour with a bit of duration. Once you've worked through the searching skills (which you will likely get through before you finish training the indication) then we can bring both elements together.

Are you happy with the stage your dog is now at? Are there any steps that you think they would benefit from working on a bit more? Make some notes below on which bits you are going to go back to.

7 STARTING SEARCHING

Before we get started on training your dog to search on cue, there are just a few general points to cover off. These will apply to all of your sessions, and whilst I may mention specifics they are worth considering when you plan your training session. First is rewarding your dog for searching. This will become more important as you move on to scent, but could also be relevant when you get to the point where your dog is searching a large area or number of items for just one or two treats. If your dog is trying hard, there is nothing wrong with quietly praising and rewarding them for searching. Try to avoid interrupting them if they are 'in the zone', but perhaps if they look to be flagging then a quick 'good dog, great work' and a treat from your hand before sending them off again can go a long way. For some dogs, searching is so inherently rewarding to them that they won't often need rewarding, but for those dogs where using their nose is less instinctive (I'm looking at you sight hounds!) then rewarding them for trying will help to build their confidence and endurance.

Next up is cheerleading… By this, I mean constantly talking to your dog whilst they're working, whether it's 'good dog', 'try over here' or 'keep at it'. I'd like you to try and avoid cheerleading. Honestly, your dog won't need it, and in some cases it could distract them from the task in hand. With cues in general, if your dog doesn't respond the first time you say your cue then it's likely they don't really know the cue as well as you think. When I send Ripley to search, I say 'search' just once. I wait to make sure that he's listening to me before I say it, but once he's been sent that's it. Imagine if you asked me to do the dishes, then stood behind me saying 'do the dishes, do the dishes' – I'm likely to be a bit confused as to why you're telling me to do something I'm already doing, and I may also be distracted from what I'm doing! I could look away from the sink, then when I turn back I won't remember if I've already wiped the plate in my hand or not. Once they've completed the search, then you can be as verbal as you like with your praise (if that's what your dog enjoys).

You have choices when your dog is doing scentwork as to whether you work with them on or off a lead. When it comes to competing, there are some of the Nosework Games where it's specified, but in general it's a personal choice. I would recommend trying both and making sure that you and your dog are comfortable with both. My experience with Ripley is that he prefers to be given the space to get on with the job, but we have done exercises to build our confidence and experience of working on a lead.

Finally, there is the difference between standing still and moving. As with working on and off lead, this is something that you will need to experiment with. To a degree you need to be consistent – either always stand still or always move. However, it's not really that black and white. This is quite a complex part of scentwork on which I will give some information as we go through the book.

There are a number of different searches that I'm going to talk you through. The process for each one is pretty similar, but there are some differences so please do read through each one. As with all aspects of scentwork, you are never 'done' with these early steps. Food searches are a great activity to do with your dog throughout their lives, and are less pressured than searching for odour. The activities covered in this section all use treats. Searching for odour will then be covered in the next section of the book, which you should only move on to once you have completed the indication training. You don't need to have worked through all the different types of searches before you move on to bringing odour in to your searches, but you should have completed all the steps of at least one of them.

Boxes and Bags

Let's get started! Try and find a quiet area where you and your dog can work without being disturbed. If you have a willing helper, talk them through the steps before you get your dog so that you are ready to go.

Step 1 – a single box

What you will need – a small box (as described in the equipment section), a number of treats

Place a single box on the floor a little way in front of your dog. Don't let them go to it just yet. If you have a helper, then you can hold on to your dog's lead whilst your helper puts the box down. With the box on the floor, place FIVE treats in and around it – one on the floor next to each outside edge and one inside. Let your dog see you doing this. Now, get a couple of treats in your hand, and get ready to release your dog. Next, say your 'search' cue to your dog. They won't know what the word means at the moment, but it's likely that they will head for the treats that they've just seen put out. You can unclip their lead, hold it loosely or drop the lead to the floor if you prefer. Watch them carefully, but try not to get in their way and avoid the temptation to point out the treats – let them use their nose!

As you see them snuffle up the last treat, use the treats in your hand to lure them away from the box. This is the time to use your new 'all done' cue – so as you put your hand with the treats under their nose, say your 'all done' cue. Try to avoid using the lead to drag them away. Using a food lure will give them a more positive experience, and create happier feelings about the searching ending.

Repeat this a few times, and watch out for your dog getting more confident and engaged in finding the treats. If they're doing really well, try putting out fewer treats so that they have to search a bit harder; still pretend to put them all down though! You can also turn your dog around before sending them to search, to try and put them off a little.

How did you and your dog get on with this? What did you see when you watched the video? Please do keep videoing your sessions.

Step 2 – adding more boxes

What you will need – at least two more boxes, a number of treats

Now that your dog is getting the idea of searching for treats in and around a box, it's time to add more boxes. First, just add in one more box so that you have two boxes down. As you did with one box, place five treats in and around each of the boxes and give your dog the search cue. Make sure to be ready with treats in your hand for when they have found all the treats. As they build in confidence, reduce the number of treats around the boxes, but every now and then make sure to put out the full ten treats. You can repeat this process with a third box, making sure that there are treats in or around all three boxes.

21 There are three boxes here, but it gives you an idea of how you could set up just one

How many boxes have you built up to? Is your dog sniffing all the way around all of them? Are they starting to respond to your 'all done' cue? They should be turning to you to collect their treat as soon as you say it. If your dog is a bit too excited, check out the 'What Should I Do If My Dog…' chapter towards the end of the book before going on to the next steps.

Step 3 – 'blank' boxes

In this step, we are going to leave a box 'blank' – this means there will be NO treats in or around that box. When you put the treats out, you still need to pretend to put treats on all the boxes – when I am training somebody and their dog, I will be speaking to the dog as I place the treats to get them excited about searching for them. Very often, the last box that you place treats at will be the first one that the dog goes to and searches. To make this exercise easier, you would make sure that there are treats on that box. To make it harder, this would be the blank box. In this step, we're building up some problem solving as well as resilience. If they don't find treats at that first box, what is their reaction? Do they give up? If so, you've possibly moved to this step too soon. If they move to the next box – great! They are learning that just because they didn't find something on that first box, it doesn't mean that there's nothing at all to find. Try not to 'cheerlead' your dog - let them work through this themselves. If you find yourself needing to frequently help them, then chances are you've moved on too quickly. There is absolutely no harm in staying at the early stages for a little bit longer; in fact, it's more likely to be beneficial.

> Remember – keep your sessions short! You shouldn't be getting through all these steps in one session. Spread them across a day or even a few days.
> TAKE YOUR TIME!

Step 4 – out of sight

Until now, your dog has seen you putting the treats on the boxes. They have a pretty good idea of where the food is before they start searching. To make it a little harder, you can turn your dog to face the other way whilst your helper puts the treats out or you can put your dog in another room whilst you set the area up. Again – mix and match, so sometimes your dog sees you put the treats out and other times they don't.

You've done all the steps with boxes for the moment – are you happy with your progress?

Step 5 – bags

Repeat the steps above with some bags. Place a couple of treats on top of the bags, as well as around the edges. The reason for doing this is to make sure that our dogs search the whole item; if they were to sniff just one corner of a box, for example, they may miss a hide (in this case a treat) that's on the opposite corner. We want to make sure that they are searching all of the items and also searching ALL OF all of the items. Remember – start with one bag, then two and finally three.

Have you covered all of the steps – what changes are you seeing in your dog? Are they getting more confident and excited about their sessions?

Step 6 – build up and combine the items

It's time to start building up the number of items. Now we can use the boxes and bags together. At most, you can use five or six boxes and five or six bags. Please build up the number gradually, and every so often go back to just one or two. As you make things harder by adding more items, make the task easier by putting treats on every item. Then you can reduce the number of treats you put out. Ultimately, you can work towards your dog searching ten to twelve boxes and bags for just one treat! And remember to sometimes let your dog see you set the area up and other times not.

> Remember – watch out for signs that your dog is tired or confused. If they are finding it hard, think about whether you've moved on too soon or if the session has been too long.
> NEVER BE AFRAID TO GO BACK ONE OR MORE STEPS!

22 Another example of a Boxes & Bags layout

Step 7 – other items

Now that your dog can confidently search boxes and bags, we're going to introduce other items. You can do this in two ways, and I recommend doing a bit of both. Firstly, you can work through all of the above steps with novel items; so start with one, then two and so on. The other option is to swap out a box or a bag for a novel item, such as a bucket or watering can. You could do this when they have a large number to search, or with a smaller number of boxes and bags. Like I say, a mixture of both approaches will be fine.

Think about what you are doing whilst your dog is searching – this is where video can be really helpful, as you probably aren't all that aware of what you're doing. If you are working your dog on a lead, is the lead long enough for them to search without you crowding them all the time? Equally, you don't want your lead to be so long that you're getting tangled up and wrapped around items. Are you moving from item to item, with your dog following you? Ideally, you want them to move between the items themselves, without you having to point everything out. Getting some independence at this stage will serve you both well as you move on. Are you standing still, with your dog just staring at you for direction? If so, you've probably moved on a bit too soon and also been helping them too much early on. Try some different strategies: stand back and send your dog into the search area, move in a zig zag pattern through the items, or walk a slow circuit around the items. Some dogs prefer us not to get involved, others like the comfort of knowing we're close by. If you are going to be in the search area, it's important to keep moving. Don't be fooled into thinking you can see more if you're standing closer: standing back can help you see the bigger picture. You need to get into the habit of observing which items your dog has and hasn't searched. You'll also need to learn how their body language changes as they catch scent – more on that later. We don't want us stopping to become a cue to the dog that they should also stop or that we're standing near the target odour.

Experiment with working both on and off lead, especially if you're in an enclosed area. A lot of communication can go along a lead, so taking it out of the picture can make a big difference. If you are using a lead, try out different lengths and types. I prefer a really light line for scentwork - I want my dog to be barely aware that it's there. It's mostly just a safety measure, and I use verbal cues to move him as needed.

There's a lot to take in here – keep taking notes and reviewing videos!

Congratulations! You've made it through the first stage of teaching your dog to search items. Don't forget, you can repeat these steps as much as you want. You should also work through them in different places. Try different rooms in your house to start with, and then take it on the road. If you're visiting friends or family why not take a couple of boxes or bags with you and see if you can spend five minutes training in their house – ask them to help out! We'll be coming back to the boxes and bags in the Bringing it All Together Chapter. You can start on that chapter once you've completed all of the above steps as well as the whole indication process. If you've not yet completed the indication steps, then carry on and try some of the other search types detailed in the following chapters. There is no rush!

8 OTHER SEARCHES

Room Searches

Room searches are a fun way to get your dog searching lots of different environments. Room searches are a great way to feed your dog their meals on rainy days! You can make them as easy or as hard as you like, depending on your dog's confidence and experience.

Step 1 – start easy

Let your dog see you place a number of treats around the edges of a room. Tuck some behind things that they can easily access, or underneath a radiator (as long as it's not on – we don't want burnt noses!). Give your search cue and let them sniff out the treats. As with the boxes, try to avoid cheerleading them – just let them sniff.

Step 2 – increase difficulty

Next time, set the treats out whilst your dog is in another room. Don't forget to watch them, and as soon as they have found the last treat give your 'all done' cue and lure them away from the search area. Have some treats on the floor, but also try to get some at nose height and maybe a little higher if your dog can safely get to them.

Step 3 – reduce the treats

By reducing the number of treats that you put out, your dog will have to work harder to get their reward. Ultimately, you could have them search the whole room for just one treat; after all, when they are on odour they could be searching for just one hide. Vary this depending on the size of the room – if you have a large room, either direct your dog to a particular section or put out a couple more treats. Don't forget to play with your dog after they have finished searching.

Searching Outside

There is an additional factor to take into consideration when searching outside – wind direction. Wind or breezes can affect inside searches if windows or doors are open, but it's generally more relevant when we're carrying out searches outside. Before asking your dog to start a search, take a moment to check which way the wind is blowing. Wind can blow scent from the source, meaning that your dog may pick it up in a completely different area. For example, the scent may be hidden on the wheel arch of the driver's side of a car. With the wind blowing across the car, your dog might pick up that scent through the wheel arch on the other side of the car. It's important that you don't instantly assume that the scent is on that side; remember the wind, and let your dog try to solve the problem. Having considered the wind, if your dog is struggling to find the source of the scent then you would be wise to take the dog around to the other side to let them search from a different angle.

Cars

I was taught to start car searches using 'sticky chicken': basically, as cheap as you can get wafer-thin chicken cut into one-inch pieces. You could also use beef or ham, or squeezy cheese.

Step 1 – one side

As we have with other searches, we'll start with the dog watching us place the treats. For the car, start with just one side of the car. Stick a few pieces of chicken at intervals along the side of the car. I prefer to start the car search using a lead to give a little control. A short distance from the car, stand with your back to the car and your dog facing you. Task them on to the corner of the car. To task your dog, start with your hand just in front of the dog's nose with your palm open and facing their nose. Sweep your hand towards your start point (the corner of the car in this case), as though you are drawing a line from your dog's nose to the start point whilst saying your 'search' cue. Allow your dog to follow your hand in a slow controlled movement. Your other hand should be holding the lead, probably quite close to the harness. As they move, allow the lead to move through your hand. I recommend that you walk backwards for the car search, with your dog coming towards you. This allows you to keep an eye on their nose! Perhaps practice this without your dog as well. As your dog comes along the side of the car they should be licking the bits of chicken off. (Your car will end up with some bits cleaner than others!) If they miss any, then you should turn around as you get to the end and come back along the car. Reset this search and repeat it a couple of times.

How did you get on with this? Walking backwards can be a little awkward – do you need to practice without your dog?

Step 2 – two sides

Next, put chicken down two consecutive sides (e.g. driver's side and front). Vary the variables by decreasing and increasing the amount of chicken. Put it at different heights, but be careful about putting it much above their head as we don't want to encourage them to put their paws up on cars. Try poking some in any little holes or grilles that you have on your car. Use the wheel arches and tyre rims. Focus on putting chicken by areas that you think hides could be put - door seals, for example.

Step 3 – all four sides

Progress to having your dog search all the way around the car. Get into the habit of going around in one direction, then turning and going back the other way. Because of wind and also the way cars are built, sometimes your dog will miss a trace of odour going in one direction but then pick it up immediately from the opposite direction. Work towards your dog being able to search the whole car for just one small bit of chicken stuck on or poked in somewhere. As always, mix this up with easier searches where there are lots of pieces to find.

Step 4 – other cars and locations

Getting to search other cars can be a little difficult if you only have access to your own, but if you have friends that are also working through this training then try to swap cars. Get someone else to set up the search for you, so that neither you nor the dog know where the treats are. Observe your dog, and see if you can see signs that they have found all the chicken. The other option is to take your car to other locations and practice the car searches.

What sort of hiding places have you found on your car? Where else have you parked your car and tried searches?

Exterior Items

At the end of the boxes and bags section I gave details about searching other items. Now you need to bring these items outside. Again, the wind will have an impact once you're searching outside. This is definitely a place where videoing and reviewing can be really helpful; watch in slow motion if needed and see if you can spot the signs of when your dog picks up on the scent of the treats.

Step 1 – three items

Start with three items that your dog is familiar working with from your indoor searches. Try to organise your items in a random fashion, and make sure to move the treats around. Try working your dog on or off lead, and get a feel for which works best for you both. Be cautious if you're not in a secure area.

Step 2 – build up items

Gradually increase the number of items until you have ten to twelve, sometimes with just one treat out. Mix up where you put treats, making sure to sometimes have them at the front, back, middle and edges.

23 Another example of an Exterior search layout

Tables and Chairs

We're coming back inside now to learn about searching tables and chairs. The process is very similar to starting out the other searches, with just a few tips to help your dog be confident in these searches. You will need a table and up to four chairs ideally, but this can easily be started with just one or two chairs. A fold up or camping table is ideal if you have access to one.

Step 1 – table and one chair

Start with the chair on its side. If you can, put the table on its side as well. Place a few treats on and around the chair and a couple under the table. Some dogs don't like going under things, and I think that the tables and chairs searches are often easier for smaller dogs. By starting with them on their sides it can make it a little less intimidating. Make sure to vary where you put the treats.

Step 2 – add in more chairs

Build up the number of chairs that you use, still having them on their side. Place the chairs on either side of your table, so that your dog has to go under or around it to complete the searching. As you did with the other searches, you can mix up whether you put treats on all of the chairs or just one of them.

24 *There are treats laid out for Ripley to search for around the upturned table and chairs*

Step 3 – stand the chairs up

You should also stand your table up at this point. Have some treats by the legs, but also a little higher including on the edge of the seat if your dog can reach there. Remember, you want them to get into the habit of searching the whole chair as the scent could be hidden anywhere on it. You could also pop treats by the table legs. In the lower levels at trials, the scent will always be on a chair, but it doesn't hurt to get them used to searching tables as well sooner rather than later.

Step 4 – different chairs and set ups

Try searching different types of chairs – rotating chairs or camping chairs, for example. Also mix up how you set up the chairs around your table, including how far they are from the table. Let your dog build up confidence going under and through the chairs.

25 An alternative layout for a Tables & Chairs search

Line Ups

Line ups are a really useful skill to teach and work on with your scentwork dog. They can be used to practice a number of different skills, and the difficulty level can be adjusted for different abilities of dogs or relevant to the element you are working on in that session.

In order to train line ups you will need five or six similar items. I have used plant pots, chairs, chocolate tubs, biscuit tins and bricks, but you can use whatever you have to hand. Different options include washing up bowls, shoes and cones. I would avoid using cardboard boxes in the first instance, as you are using them for the boxes and bags searches and we don't want to cause any confusion.

We are going to be working line ups with your dog on a lead, and I would recommend using a harness in order to avoid pressure on the neck. Make sure that the harness is non-restrictive and doesn't tighten on the dog in any way if they pull into it. I only have one

dog at the moment, but of course he has at least five harnesses...
Having a harness specifically for scentwork can help to get your
dog into the 'sniffing' frame of mind - they start to learn that
when the lead is attached to this particular harness, then they are
going to be asked to start searching.

Step 1 – one item

We'll be starting with just one item. For the sake of talking
through the steps, I'm going to use plant pots in my examples.
Place your pot upside down on the ground, and pop a few treats
on and around it (much like we did when we started with one
box). Task your dog to the item; good practice is to pretend that
there is an item before the first one you're searching as well as one
after it – so rather than pointing directly at the first item, aim your
hand to the ground slightly ahead of it. This will make sure that
your dog gets into the habit of searching the full line and not
trying to cut away too soon. To task your dog, start with your
hand just in front of the dog's nose with your palm open and
facing their nose. Sweep your hand towards your start point (so
the ground a little way in front of the plant pot in this case), as
though you are drawing a line from your dog's nose to the start
point. Say your 'search' cue at the same time. Allow your dog to
follow your hand in a slow controlled movement. Your other
hand should be holding the lead, probably quite close to the
harness. As they move, allow the lead to move through your
hand. With line ups you want to give the dog enough lead to be
able to search the items, but not so much that they can race ahead.
If you allow them to race ahead, then there's a chance that they
will miss items in their rush. This exercise is really about
methodical searching.

Leads – I like to use a really light line for scentwork. The dog is less likely to be distracted by the weight of the lead. I try not to use the lead to move the dog, rather using verbal cues or food lures.

Step 2 – adding more items

I would recommend moving from one item to three, as it gives more flexibility for building variety in to the search. Start out by putting treats on all three, then switch to putting treats on just two or one then back to all three. Vary those variables! Try to avoid getting into a pattern of always putting treats on one particular plant pot. We don't want your dog to learn a pattern, we want them to learn to search every item and to search all of every item. Aim to keep the speed down; don't forget that this should be a methodical search. Once they are confidently searching three items then build up to five or six.

26 There are treats on the pots to encourage Ripley to search them

Step 3 – different items

Work line ups with different items. If you have space, then put out more than one line. Remember to mix up whether there are treats on all of the items or just some of them. I would suggest putting treats on the first item more frequently than some of the others, as lots of dogs will be in such a rush to get going that they will overshoot that first item. Frequently loading it will get them in the habit of always checking that first item. As with when there was just one item, work the line as if there is an item before the first and another after the last.

Step 4 – blank lines

Occasionally include blank lines in your training. This means no treats on any of the items. If you decide to compete, then there could be times when there are no hides – introducing this concept in training helps to keep your dog's confidence in searching. When you do a blank line, you will need to reward your dog at the end; this reinforces them for searching and helps to make them feel OK about NOT finding anything. To start with, only work the line in one direction before rewarding. Avoid working blank lines repetitively; we don't want the dog to start thinking that there's no point searching as the reward won't come until the end. You can progress to working a blank line in both directions. Again, don't overdo this and intersperse blank lines with lines where there are treats to find.

9 BRINGING IT ALL TOGETHER

By now you should have worked through all of the steps for an indication, plus at least one of the searches. Your dog should be confidently searching a number of items for treats, and they should have some duration with their nose hold on a scented tin. Now we will bring the two parts together, so that your dog will learn to search items for the target odour. We'll be starting with the tin, and then I'll run through each of the searches giving some ideas and tips for each of them.

Hiding the Tin

For this you will need your tin which should have a scented soak in it. You can also use blank tins if you have space.

Step 1 – tin in sight

Up until this point, the tin has been near to you, and most likely your dog has been coming towards you to indicate on it. Now they will learn to go away from you to get to it as well. You're going to put the tin somewhere that the dog should still be able to see it as they approach - just behind a sofa or tucked behind a bin, for example. To start with, let them see you place it. Send them from a short distance away, and you should now use your 'search' cue. Mark them as soon as they get to it – don't hold out for any sort of duration yet. Once you've done a couple of repetitions, move on to the next step.

Step 2 – tin out of sight

Now you need to hide your tin as best you can – this can be a little harder with a large tin, but you could incorporate this step into a boxes and bags search. I'll give a bit more detail on that later. For now, see if you can tuck it a little further behind some furniture, or you could put it in a cupboard and leave the door open a little. Make sure that the holes in the tin are facing up or out. You also want to make sure that your dog doesn't see you placing the tin. From now on your scented hides will be 'blind' for your dog: they're not going to know where they are. Bring your dog into the search area and ask them to search. Try to avoid giving them clues; in other words, don't stand facing the hide! Move around whilst they're searching, and KEEP MOVING even once they've found it. Try to give your marker whilst your feet are still moving. The reason for this is that dogs can start to pick up on little signals from you; if you stand still as they approach the hide then they will soon start to think that anytime you stand still they must be getting close. We don't want that.

I know there's a lot to take in there, so I will reiterate the importance of video. When you review your videos, you will be able to better see what subtle signals your dog is responding to as well as seeing what you are actually doing whilst they are searching. Learn to really observe your dogs and pick up on the changes in their body language that mean they are 'on odour'. Cloves are known to be a 'big' odour – many dogs (and some humans!) can smell it as soon as they enter a search area. The skill is in getting to the source of that odour. I promised to avoid too much technical information, so if you want to find out more about how odour works in general then do please look into it.

What sort of places have you hidden your tin? Is your dog starting to pick up that the 'search' cue now means they are looking for the scented tin?

As your dog builds in confidence on this step then you can hold out for a bit more duration on your indication. Alternatively, try bigger search areas. Don't change both criteria at the same time though; if you use a bigger search area then stick to marking immediately to start with.

Working through the above two steps will start to pair your search cue with finding odour. We will be cementing this as we work through each of the different searches using scent.

Boxes and Bags

Before working through these next steps you should have completed all of the steps in the Boxes and Bags section as well as all of the indication steps. You could work on the below steps at the same time as the hiding the tin steps above, but NOT in the same session.

Step 1 – tin in or by box

The easiest way to introduce scent to your boxes and bags search is by using the tin that your dog is already familiar with from the indications training. Start out with three boxes, and build up to five. Do the same with three to five bags, and finally your combined boxes and bags. With the three boxes, place your tin behind one of the boxes to start. Don't let your dog see you doing this. Bring your dog into the area and give your 'search' cue. Up until this point, they've always found treats in this scenario so it may be a little confusing for them initially. Watch how they behave; are they sniffing all the boxes as they have in the past? Are they sniffing all the way around all of the boxes? They should get to the tin quite quickly as there are only three boxes; watch their reaction. You will be wanting to mark immediately as their nose gets to the tin for the first few tries. This will help to cement the association between the search cue, the scent and treats. When you watch your video back (because you are videoing, aren't you?), can you see a change in their body language as they either see the tin or catch its odour? The more you observe, the more you'll be able to read what point of the search your dog is at. I love watching all sorts of dogs searching, as they all have different tells. If you do decide to try competing with your dog, I would highly recommend volunteering to help at trials as you get to watch different dogs and really hone your observation skills. This then transfers to your own training.

You could also put the tin inside one of the boxes, to make sure that your dog is sniffing in there. Perhaps lift one of the flaps and poke the tin under there. Or lay the boxes on their sides. If your dog is getting really confident, then pick a box that has some gaps and place the tin UNDER it. Now your dog will definitely need to use their nose! Making it harder like that, ensure you mark as soon as they show interest in the correct box. By marking quickly, you should avoid the risk of the dog trying to trash the box to get to the tin or soak. Remember your careful scent handling – I would now consider this box 'hot' or contaminated. Either stick to using that one box for hides (this is easiest if you have a number of identical boxes) or dispose of it and rotate in a clean box.

You can either repeat the above with your bags and then combine with the boxes until your dog can find the tin with ten to twelve boxes and bags out, or you can move to just using soaks. Or a combination. Tins are handy for putting out quick hides in lots of different places. And you can do a few quick hand-held indications as well.

Step 2 – using soaks

Again, we're going to start out with just three boxes, but move fairly quickly to five. It's helpful if you have a few identical or very similar boxes (e.g. wine boxes or shoe boxes) as you don't want your dog to learn the particular box that the scent is always in. It also saves having to have lots of boxes, because you could only use it a couple of times before having to rotate it out. Start by placing the soak right by a gap on the box – if the box is open, then just underneath the flap for example. You should scent your box up, set up the search and leave it for five to ten minutes before asking your dog to search. Make sure they can't see you setting it all up though! The longer you leave it, the more the scent will dissipate around the room. This can add a level of difficulty, so don't leave it for too long to start with.

Cue your dog to search – watch their body language for signs that they've picked up on the odour and see how they work towards the source of it. When they get to the correct box, give them time to get as close as they can to where the soak is; this is known as 'going to source' and is a really important skill. I'll be covering off some ideas later on how to train that. However, don't leave it too long, and don't wait for any sort of duration of indication. As soon as you consider that they are close enough, go ahead and mark them. Reward them well – this is getting harder now!

> Are you still using play in your training? I do hope so! Now that we're increasing the difficulty, the relief and joy of play will be even more important.

Step 3 – build up the items

Switch around whether you scent up a box or a bag, and also vary whereabouts you put the scented item in the search area. Set things up in such a way that your dog gets a mixture of quick finds and ones where he has to search the whole area. Vary whether you put out a full ten to twelve item search or just three to five items.

Step 4 – other items

Just as we faded other items into the treat searches, so we can with searches for scent. Don't go over the ten to twelve item limit for now though. Remember to try these searches in different rooms in the house.

Step 5 – increase the number of hides

This step isn't strictly necessary, especially if you are working on scentwork just for fun. However, if you do decide to compete, then at Level 2 and above in Scentwork UK there will be more than one scented item in a search area and there are multiple hides in most of the Nosework Games. I would advise sticking to two to start with, and remove the first hide once they've found it. Getting to multiple hides is more of an advanced skill that's outside the scope of this book.

Room Searches

Now that your dog knows the target odour of cloves, you can ask them to search a room or part of a room for scent. You could do this by progressing your tin hides, or you could put soaks out. Just be aware of the risk of leaving residue odour, so either alternate the rooms that you use or make use of containers for your soaks. I only really have two rooms at home that I can use for searches, so I generally make sure my soaks are contained. If we are ensuring that we only ever mark and reward our dogs for being at the source of the odour then residue shouldn't be a big problem, but we want to avoid that confusion if we can.

Step 1 – start easy

Make sure that the first few hides you put out are at a height that is easy for your dog to find as well as in a simple location. Thinking about a kitchen as an example, you could put a hide at nose height just poking out of a cupboard door. The handy thing about kitchen cupboards is that they can be disinfected afterwards to remove any residue odour. As with the boxes search, make sure to either stand still and be neutral OR keep moving as your dog searches and as they find the scent. MARK ON THE MOVE! I will often do a couple of easy room searches on days that we haven't had a long walk, just so that Ripley gets an extra chance to use his nose.

Step 2 – make it harder

Your imagination and room availability are your limits here – I can guarantee you'll be sat watching the TV in the evening, glancing around the room for hidey holes. In my living room we have a log store and wine rack that both make excellent hiding places. Mix up the height of the hides to make sure that your dog is searching both high and low. If your dog is allowed on furniture, then you can really ramp up the challenge by having the hide somewhere that requires them to do this. Not an option for Ripley… Set up barriers; maybe put a chair in front of where the hide is so that they have to work out how best to get to source. Ripley tends towards taking the most direct route, whether that be over, under or through! Other dogs will be more cautious in their approach. Room searches are a great way of introducing problem solving challenges into your dog's scentwork.

Cars

Don't forget the effect of wind on your searching outside; it's more important than ever to remember that now that we're introducing scent.

Step 1 – the only step, really!

Making sure to follow your careful scent handling procedures, hide a soak on the car. The easiest options are to trap it in a door trim, poke it behind a number plate or put it in a hole or grille. You don't want your dog watching you whilst you place the scent. Best practice is to leave it for at least ten minutes before you bring your dog out to search; head inside and have a cup of tea! This allows the odour to circulate - if you ever take your dog to a scent trial then you will never be working on freshly placed scent. It will have been sitting for at least ten minutes, and if you are late in the running order then it could have been there for a couple of hours. It's worth bearing this in mind when you are training. When you bring your dog out to search, remember to walk backwards and work the car in both directions if they don't find it on the first pass. Don't hold out for a lengthy indication in your first few searches; mark and have a party as soon as they hit the scent.

27 Working his way along the side of the car to a hide in the door seal

Make sure you practice your car searches in different places, and always be mindful of that wind. Try to set up your searches with that in mind to help your dog learn how to work the wind. That will be easier for some than others; I have spaniels, and they do have a natural ability to work the wind.

<u>Walls</u>

If you decide to try out a Scentwork UK trial, then you may come across a wall search either in combination with a car or on its own. The length of the wall you search could be between 10m and 40m. Once you start doing wall searches, you will spot walls everywhere that you'd like to search! As wall searches were added after I'd already been training scentwork for a while, we went ahead and trained on odour straight away. That's not to say that you couldn't train wall searches with food, but it is a little harder as there will be difficulty attaching food to walls…

Step 1 – short wall

Pick a short piece of wall, maybe just five metres long. Tuck a soak into a crack or hole somewhere along the wall. As with the car, at this stage try to avoid putting it above head height. For your early searches, start with it at nose height as your dog is most likely to hit that. However, move fairly quickly to varying the height so that they learn they have to search high and low. Like you did with the car search, start with working this one on a lead and with you walking backwards a little out from the wall. This will allow you to make sure that your dog searches every inch of the wall and to see any changes that indicate they've picked up odour. Consider the wall like a long car; walk it in one direction and then back the other.

> If your soak isn't contained, then remember there will be residual odour. You should avoid that search area for a few days and/or clean the area if possible.

28 This wall has lots of great holes to tuck hides into

Step 2 – longer walls

Gradually build up to searching longer walls. Vary whether the hide is near the start, middle or end as well as at different heights. Remember that the wind could have an impact on where your dog will pick up the odour. Observe them! You will start to see signs of when your dog has picked up the scent – let them work, and as in the other searches avoid using your lead to move them.

29 I stay back, but keep moving as Ripley searches

Step 3 – corners

Dogs have a habit of cutting corners, and many handlers let them! You want your dog to get into the habit of working all the way into and out of corners, as there may be a hide there. This is something you can practice with treats; lay a trail of treats into the corner and out again. Give your dog space on corners, as part of their reluctance could be linked to pressure and the sense of being trapped. Make sure to put hides in corners so that your dog learns that they really need to be searched. Hone your observation skills; watch your dog work the wall and mentally note any bits they show extra interest in or miss. If needed you can then go back and specifically task them in those areas.

Step 4 – other challenges

There are a couple of different challenges that I have come across in trials that I can suggest looking for. One was a narrow area with a wall either side (actually, I was the judge here and as it was Level 2 I was able to set a hide on either side). The gap was path width at the back of a building. One of the challenges here was for those working on a lead or line, especially with larger dogs. But it was also hard for those with dogs off lead to try and get the space needed to observe their dog searching. It's definitely worth practising in narrow spaces to make sure your dog is comfortable in that environment. The other challenge I came across in a trial was a split wall; this was combined with a vehicle search on this occasion. So there was one length of wall behind the car, then the car and another length of wall in front of the car. You could practice this sort of set up with or without a car. Vary those variables!

Tables and Chairs

As mentioned when I introduced you to searching tables and chairs, in the early stages the scent should always be on a chair. When you are scenting your chair, make sure to vary where you put the scent; start with it on an edge under the seat part, progress to putting it under a foot. Scent under the foot of a chair is quite a hard one for most dogs, so don't be in a rush to get to that. Also vary how far the chair is pushed under the table as well as the position around a table. I've even come across a search where the chairs were facing outwards, so don't forget to try that!

Line Ups

Step 1 – one line

You will only have one scented item in your line, but you can move the item within the line. Make sure to move the scented item, NOT just the soak. We don't want to cause any confusion by potentially having residual scent on an item. If you are attaching the soak directly to an item, make sure that you mark the item in some way – remember the advice given about scent handling! Start with a short line of just three items, building up to five or six. Don't forget to work the invisible items at the start and end of the line.

Step 2 – multiple lines

If you have enough space, and enough items, then you can work on a number of lines. You could include a blank line, remembering to reward your dog for searching even though they didn't find anything. Make sure to have the hide in the first item sometimes so that your dog learns that it's worth searching everything and doesn't get into the habit of skipping items. Stick to working Line Ups on a lead, and as with the car and wall searches it can be helpful to walk backwards a little way in front of your dog.

Step 3 – reinforcing indications

Line Ups can be a great way of reinforcing indications with your dog; you can mark as soon as they hit the right item, or you can hold out for a bit of duration if that's the aim of your session. Try to pick items that are easy to indicate on if you are working on this skill.

Using Line Ups is also a great way of introducing a new scent; you can start by pairing with food (i.e. put a treat on the item that is scented) and quickly move to just marking quickly as they hit the scented item before waiting for a solid indication with duration. However, you should only work on one skill at a time with your Line Ups. So if you want to introduce a new scent, don't also plan to increase duration of indication. If you're working on getting them systematically searching every item, don't do it with a new scent. Decide on the focus for your session and make all the other elements as easy as possible. As with the other searches, and probably even more importantly with Line Ups – MARK ON THE MOVE! If you happen to come to a standstill as soon as they get to the scented item, then you will soon find that they will start indicating on whatever item they are close to every time you stand still, whether it's scented or not.

Next Steps

Below I will go over a final few things to consider adding in to your sessions to complete your scentwork training.

Calling the find – if you decide to compete in scentwork, then you will need to be able to let the judge know when you think your dog has found the scented item. This is known as 'calling the find', and should happen BEFORE you mark your dog. It's a skill that you will need to practise, and I would recommend regularly pretending to call the find in your training sessions. There are a few different ways of calling the find; raising a hand, saying something like 'find' or 'alert' or a combination of the two. I generally just raise my hand these days, as that tends not to distract Ripley from holding his indication on the find. As soon as the judge confirms the find I can use my clicker or marker word to let Ripley know he's won some treats. I would avoid calling the alert using your marker word. Let's take the example of your marker word being 'yes' – you task your dog to search, and they indicate on an item. You say 'yes' to let the judge know that you think they've found the scented item. However, they have alerted on an incorrect object (there are a number of reasons why this can happen, some of which will be covered in a later chapter). You've told your dog that they are correct, and should then give them a reward. Now if you give that reward, you have reinforced them for indicating incorrectly. If you DON'T give the reward, you're eroding the value of your marker. Neither of these is ideal, so definitely consider training with an alternative call. Until this point, your marker has acted as a release from the indication; basically, giving them permission to move. Now they will need to learn to pay a little more attention to your words! You could compete without training this element, but it will save confusion for your dog if you prepare them as well as you can; we want to be as clear to them as we can.

Step 1 – easy search

Set up an easy search with just a few items. Alternatively, you could use one of the Going to Source set ups detailed below. As your dog is indicating, either raise your hand or say your 'find' or 'alert' word. This should be pretty soon after your dog starts indicating, no duration at the moment. Chances are, your dog will move away from their indication. Don't say anything, just wait and see what they do. If they return to indicating on the scent, then once again try calling the find and then very quickly marking them.

Step 2 – add a pause

Repeat as above, but gradually increase the time between calling the find and marking. You want to get to the sort of time span that would allow a judge to confirm that they are correct.

Blind searches – these are searches where you don't know where the hide is. To be honest, they are next to impossible to set up if you are training alone so you will need someone to help out. Working blind searches will help you to really hone your observation skills, as your only clue as to the location of the hide is your dog's body language and behaviour. I used to really worry about the fact that I didn't get to practice many blind searches, but have since learned the value of working known hides so am less concerned. That said, if you are thinking about competing then you will want to practice some blind hides before you do. Make sure that whoever is helping you has had some instruction in clean scent handling if they aren't already familiar with scentwork. To make it easier for both of you, perhaps consider using something like Line Ups to start with, where you can scent an item and then your helper can just swap the items around without needing to touch the scent. Get your helper to place all the items out, as we need their scent to be on all the items; this ensures that your dog is alerting on the target odour, and not on the helper's scent. The only difference between the scented item and all of the others should be the target odour – remember to include your non-scented sock pieces when setting hides.

Don't forget to incorporate your new 'calling the find' skill – you're not going to know if your dog is right until your helper confirms it!

Other scents – your dog is capable of learning a number of different scents. With Scentwork UK, the other two scents they use are Gun Oil and Truffle Oil. You can find details of how to prepare the odour on their website. I use the scent tin and then some Go to Source exercises (covered in the next chapter) to introduce the new scent.

Step 1 - Start by putting a soak from your new scent jar in a clean tin (i.e. one that hasn't been used for cloves). Present the tin to your dog and mark as soon as their nose touches it. Repeat this a number of times, delaying a little as you progress.

Step 2 – If you have a few tins, then add a couple more to the search so that your dog has to make a choice – mark quickly to start with to give them confidence.

Step 3 – As you did when we first started bringing everything together, hide the tin and let your dog search. By now they will be starting to understand that this new scent is relevant so you should start to see their indication getting stronger.

Step 4 – Use the new scent in searches (easy ones to start with), as well as some of the Go to Source exercises and Line Ups.

10 ADDITIONAL SKILLS

This chapter is broken down in to two sections: Going to Source and Ripley's Sniffing Games.

Going to Source

Going to Source is the difference between a dog indicating that the scent is on a particular chair and them indicating exactly where on the chair the scent is. By focusing on training our dogs to go to source, we give ourselves a margin of error when and if we decide to try a competition. With some of the searches, such as the car or wall search, the dog needs to be within six inches of where the scent is to be awarded the find. This also applies in all the searches at higher levels. Go to Source exercises are also a great way of building understanding and duration in your dog's indication. I have taught entire workshops on going to source in the past, and have an online version available through a Facebook group. I won't be going into all of the details of that in this book, but will share a few exercises you can use to build on this skill.

Musical chair – this is probably my favourite, as it's a quick and easy one to do with just one chair. The idea here is that the scent stays in one place, but you move the chair around. If you have enough space, you can also vary the angle that your dog approaches from. Get your chair set up in the middle of a room, with the scent in an easy spot for your dog to find and indicate on. On a corner just under the seat is a good spot. Bring your dog in and cue them to search. The focus here is to get them to source, so once you see that they are there, mark and REWARD AT SOURCE. Cup one hand just by the scent and place treats from your other hand in there for your dog to eat. Then take a treat and toss it away from the chair for your dog to chase. As they go, turn the chair around. You could also turn it upside down or put it on its side. As your dog returns, cue them immediately to search if needed – I don't generally need to cue again once we've started this game. Repeat this five or six times, always remembering to reward at source and move the chair around each time. Finish your session with a bit of play as usual. Once your dog has the hang of this game, then you can start to wait for a bit of duration on the indication – this is a great game for building understanding and duration of the indication.

Big box – a long, tall box is ideal for this game or you could use any other larger item that you can easily move around. The process is basically the same as with the musical chair. Mark and reward at source and move the box around as you send your dog after a reset treat.

Jelly pots – I bought some jelly moulds that work perfectly for this exercise, and my husband helpfully made a board for them to slot in to! You could use a muffin tin, in which case you will need your scent in a container of some sort (one small enough to fit in a muffin tin). The other option is the spice tins. This is basically a variation of the work you did with tins when building the indication. I usually do this with six pots as shown in the picture below. These pots have removable bottoms, and my scent is stuck to the bottom of the red one. I usually have this on the floor at my feet, between me and my dog. I'll cue him to search, and wait until his nose is in the correct pot – again, I may use this set up to build on his indication behaviours. Once I've marked, I will cup one hand over the correct pot and feed his treats to him there.

Throw a reset treat, and either turn the whole board around or pull out the scented pot and swap it with a clean one. Repeat this five or six times before stopping for a play break. Lift the board off the floor at this point. If you're using a muffin tin, then just move the scented container between the holes; ideally you should have empty containers in the other holes to ensure your dog isn't just using his eyes.

30 Jelly moulds in a wooden board

Bricking it – Bricks are usually pretty easy and cheap to get hold of. There are lots of styles that have handy holes in them. Place a number together and work in a similar way to the jelly pots above. Your easiest option here is going to be using the scent in a small container of some sort.

When working through these set ups, vary whether you mark immediately or whether you hold out for a bit of duration. Some of these are also easy to take on the road and play in different places. This is great for generalising your training, and they can also be useful for helping your dog to settle in new places. You could even look out for natural places to train this whilst you're out on your walks!

Ripley's Sniffing Games

Below are some examples of a few different sniffing games that we play from time to time. You can find videos of these in the Scentwork Online Challenges group on Facebook. I won't go into detail about how to train each one, but will add in some helpful tips. Hopefully they will inspire you to try some different things.

High and Low – as simple as it sounds, try setting hides at different heights. This was also touched on when I covered Room Searches, but can be kept in mind for wherever you set out a search.

Shoes – set out a load of different shoes and hide the scent in one of them. If your scent is in a container you can just swap the container to different shoes after each find, or you can move the shoes around. Lay the shoes close together and use them as a Going to Source exercise. Shoes can be great for helping to build some duration into your indication – just remember to pick one skill to work on at a time.

Blocking – this means standing in the way of the hide, so that your dog has to get past you to get to it. This is something that handlers often do unintentionally in trial situations, and so is definitely a skill worth practicing. Your dog needs to learn that just because you're stood in front of something it doesn't mean it shouldn't be searched. The exception to this is when they are searching for multiple hides within one search area, and have already found the one you're standing in front of. Start easy by ensuring there is space for them to get around you, and build up as their confidence grows.

Distance – how far can you send your dog to search? As with other skills, start easy and build up. This is one where you will need to be able to stand still whilst your dog searches.

Distraction scents – distraction scents come up in the higher levels of Scentwork UK. They include coffee, toothpaste, vanilla essence and almond essence. They can be prepared by putting a few drops on a cotton makeup pad. This should then be hidden on one of your items, with your target odour being on another item. Keep a good distance between these items to start with. There is every chance that your dog will show interest in the distraction scent at first; just ignore them. If they indicate, or really get stuck, then call them away and make the search a bit easier. Perhaps incorporate the distraction scent into a Line Up or Going to Source game where you can set things up so that they hit the target odour first a few times before changing things so that they come across the distraction scent first. Some distraction scents will be harder than others due to their similarity to our target scent. We want our dogs to learn that the only scent that matters is the one we have taught them.

Other distractions - this will vary from dog to dog. Vinnie's favourite thing in the whole world was tennis balls, so setting a search up with a load of tennis balls scattered around was TOUGH. As it was, he would pick up and carry one ball then carry on searching until he found the hide. He was a multi-tasking expert, and could do nearly anything with a tennis ball or two in his mouth. As I've touched on before, Ripley loves to retrieve and so putting out a lot of toys that he is used to retrieving, and then hiding scent in one of them was a real challenge. Could he indicate with a nose freeze on a toy that he would just love to pick up? Well, after a little practice, yes he could. He really understands what his 'search' word means: find the target odour and stick your nose on it until I give a release cue. Have a think about what would be distracting for your dog and build that into your searches. Next for Ripley will be food; I'll be starting by having that food contained so that he can't just help himself, then will make it harder as I can see his confidence grow.

Water – the thing that most dogs I've seen find hardest about water searches is how to indicate – they don't want to get their noses wet! One way to help with this is to start with a cover on your containers. You can also mark early so that they learn they can hold their head just above the water line. I was cynical about whether my dogs could find a hide that was under water, but they absolutely can! You can try this as a line up or as a free search.

Hanging hides - these are so much fun, as they just won't stay still as the dog tries to indicate! You could start with items hanging next to a wall, so there is something for them to stop against or even tape them in such a way to reduce the swinging about. Progress to hanging off a frame or anything else that you can tie a bit of string to. You can use socks, cups, plant pots or the jelly pots from Going to Source.

11 WHAT SHOULD I DO IF MY DOG…

Every dog is unique, we all know that. Following a series of steps for a training process should work for most dogs, but there are always going to be things that happen along the way that throw us off and leave us wondering what we should do. I've tried to pick out a few things below that could come up, in the hope they will help anyone who comes across them. However, there is every chance that I will miss something so please make use of the resources detailed at the back of the book for further support, or get in touch with any questions. I'll always do my best to help if I can.

Fancy footwork – when training the indication, your dog starts to paw at the pot or your hand. If this happens, don't say anything; no 'ah-ah' and no pushing the foot away. Just quietly put the pot behind your back. This removes their access to reinforcement – they can't get a treat if the pot isn't there! Bring the pot back around and be sure to mark quickly as their nose goes in the pot. Use this strategy whenever they try to get their foot involved. Very often this sort of thing will creep back in as we raise criteria or change anything, for example when you move from having the pot at nose height to lowering it.

Barking – there are a number of reasons why dogs bark during training, or at any other time for that matter. Some dogs just like the sound of their own voice… Often in training barking is a sign of frustration, and so we may need to take a step back and consider what is causing that frustration. Similar to the approach with their feet above, we can try removing the access to reinforcement, but that may cause more frustration. So you really need to know your dog with this one; video may be helpful to see what triggers them into barking mode. If they're barking, they probably aren't thinking clearly so take a break and come back to it another time.

Overexcitement – some dogs get very excited about training and interacting with us. They can then be further excited about access to novel items and food. For these dogs, start with just one item and alternate this item with others each time you do a session. Also consider using lower value treats; Ripley doesn't really think about what he's doing if I have high value treats such as dried sausages or fresh meat. For him I get more done if I use less exciting treats such as kibble for most of our training. I can then use the higher value treats at the end of sessions for our food play. Once they can interact relatively calmly with one item, add another and slowly build from there. Any time they start to get excited, call them away from the search area and do some slow strokes along their body to help them bring their energy level down.

My dog just stares at me – this is most likely to crop up near the start of your training journey, and possibly because your dog is used to being 'told' what to do. Make the exercises as easy as you need to ensure that they can succeed. Use high value treats for the searching to tempt them into sniffing. It can also happen when you make things a little harder, almost like they give up. This can be because you've moved on too soon, so go back a step and try and progress in smaller increments. However, it can also happen if you've not moved on soon enough. Your dog has been used to succeeding by doing a particular behaviour, and now that's not working – look for progress, not perfection, to avoid this.

Struggling to build duration – there is an additional process you can go through to try and help build duration in your dog's indication: you can incorporate a chin rest. The easiest way to teach a chin rest is to cup your dog's chin in your hand and rapidly feed a number of treats. Repeat this a few times, and then hold your hand just a tiny bit away from their chin and wait for them to lower it into your hand; feed rapid fire treats. Once your dog is lowering their chin into your hand, start to slow down the treats and pause briefly between them. Alternate between rapid fire and pausing. Next, you can combine your chin rest with your pot; hold your pot in your cupped hand that your dog has just had a lot of treats for resting their chin in. You can then either mark as they rest their chin in the pot, or feed directly into the pot if you've cut a hole in it.

False alerts – false alerts or indications are where your dog indicates on the incorrect item. This can happen for a number of reasons: your dog may be worried by the environment and sees indicating as the quickest way of getting out of it, or they may be picking up on your body language. Video will be helpful here, as on reviewing you may spot what caused the indication. Make use of Line Ups and Going to Source exercises to reinforce alerting on the correct items.

12 SUMMARY

Well, here we are at the end of the book – did you enjoy it? I do hope so. I also hope that you've started working on the exercises in the book, and that both you and your dog are having fun.

I started out explaining why you would want to do scentwork, and a little bit about how our dog's noses work. I also talked about the different options you have for progressing as well as touching on the benefits of going back to basics from time to time. As a reminder, the two organisations that I have experience of competing with are Scentwork UK and Nosework Games. Their websites give all the details of the searches you might encounter. They also have supportive Facebook pages where you can ask questions. If you work through the progressions in this book, then you're most of the way towards being ready to try and compete.

Once we'd established the benefits of scentwork it was time to think about the equipment that we might need, and get it all together to be ready to start training. This also included treats; thinking about using the right treats for our dog, and also making sure that they wouldn't gain too much weight during training. Linked closely to treats was the brief explanation of clicker training. I didn't cover this in detail, but I would suggest looking at the reference section for further resources if you would like to learn more about this method of training. Next up in that section was play – I hope by now that you are incorporating more play into your interactions with your dog. Finally, I covered scent preparation and handling; I gave you the details of how to get your scent jars ready. Remember to keep your jar topped up with soaks, and you'll want to refresh the cloves every ten to twelve weeks. As you progress, you can add other items to your jar to use as soaks; felt dots are great, but try out other materials as well. You can also get different containers for holding your soaks for hides. This can save residual scent getting on items that you use for hides. Check out the suppliers listed at the back of the book.

Then the fun began! I started by covering the steps needed to teach an indication. There's a lot to this skill, but it's well worth putting the time in. You can also re-visit the early steps at any time in your training journey. Next, it was time to learn about how to teach your dog to search (and when to stop). Remember, even once your dog is searching for target odour, you can go back to these early exercises for fun and to fine tune your searching.

Finally, I talked through bringing it all together. Getting your dog searching for a target odour, and indicating that they've found it. Party time! Now you can get out in the world and practise this wherever you go with your dog. Sometimes easy, sometimes harder. Get family or friends to put out hides and show off your dog's new skills. Most of all – HAVE FUN!

I would love to hear how you got on with the book. What was your favourite exercise, and are you enjoying your scentwork journey? You can find my contact details in the next section. If you would like some more ideas of scent games to play, then I created a Scentwork Online Challenges Facebook Group during the pandemic lockdown in early 2020. Feel free to join the group and give the challenges a try. You can post video there if you're comfortable to do so.

References and Resources

You can find out more about Scentwork UK on their website, www.scentworkuk.com or the Scentwork UK Facebook Group.

Nosework Games also have a website, www.noseworkgames.uk and Facebook Page.

Fenzi Dog Sports Academy, www.fenzidogsportsacademy.com – a huge variety of resources, including webinars, workshops and six-week courses.

When Pig Dogs Fly – Jane Killion (one of the easiest to understand resources I have read about clicker/positive reinforcement training).

Kikopup YouTube channel – excellent examples of clicker training in action.

JR Pet Products have a huge range of natural treats, www.jrpetproducts.com

Scentdog for scent supplies, www.scentdog.co.uk/shop

Connect with the Author

Have you enjoyed the book? Would you like to stay in touch with me, and continue your scentwork journey? Amazing!

Here are my social media links:

Facebook - Compass Canine Scentwork
Ripley has his own Instagram and Facebook pages, both called Talented Mr Rip
Scentwork Online Challenges Facebook Group
You can find further videos on my YouTube Channel

Visit my website:

www.compasscanine.co.uk

If you'd like to sign up to the Self Study Facebook course that inspired this book, you can find the details on the website above. For updates, please subscribe to my mailing list using the link which can be found on the website above.

Made in the USA
Columbia, SC
28 March 2024